Grief Doesn't Have the Last Word

The promise of blessing in seasons of sorrow

Pastor Kurt Ebert

Published by Straight Talk Books
P.O. Box 301, Milwaukee, WI 53201
800.661.3311 · timeofgrace.org

Printed in the United States of America

ISBN: 978-1-942107-09-5

―――――

My 16-year-old son Nathan unexpectedly took his own life. It is my prayer that whatever grief may have touched the lives of God's children, the Lord will continue to fulfill his promise to sanctify and bless them through and through.

―――――

Contents

I Don't Understand God's Ways—And That's Okay

As believers, we celebrate the truth that our God has revealed a portion of his name and glory to all who will seek him in his Word. We confess him as the triune God—the Father, Son, and Holy Spirit, three persons united in one Godhead, coequal, coeternal, comajestic. Wow! What a God! But I truly don't understand him, do you? I can draw diagrams and seek to explain what Scripture says using word pictures, but to truly understand him . . . no, that knowledge is reserved for God himself.

But I don't need to understand him to trust him. In fact, I'm kind of glad to have a God so big, so complex, so otherworldly that I *don't* understand him or his ways. If I could really comprehend his essence, his reasoning, his plans, and his actions— well, then, wouldn't he be a lot like me? I don't need another me when my heart is being torn to pieces. I'm glad to have One I can't fathom. That kind of God I can trust.

One Who Knew

That was a blessing and a lesson that Job came to learn too. Do you know Job from the Bible? He was a fabulously wealthy and blessed man, highly respected in his day. At a time when wealth was measured in animals, he had thousands of camels, cattle, donkeys, and goats. Hundreds of paid servants called him master. On top of all that, he had a wife and ten children—seven sons and three daughters. People honored him and came to him for advice. And it seemed he didn't let his prosperity go to his head. He was an upright and godly man who prayed for his children and even offered sacrifices on their behalf in case they had partied a bit too enthusiastically together. He shared his wealth with those less fortunate. The Lord smiled on him. He was considered the greatest man of his time. In the eyes of others, you could say he "had it all."

But then it all changed. God did something no human being can ever really comprehend: he talked to Satan. It looks like God allowed Satan to force his hand and get him to give permission to the tempter to afflict Job. "Sure he follows you," Satan goaded the Lord. "Why shouldn't he? You've put a hedge around his life and kept anything bad from touching him. But it's all a facade, a relationship made of paper-mache. Just touch his life with a bit of pain and watch it unravel. I predict he'll curse you to your face" (see Job 1:9–11).

God permitted Satan his argument and allowed him to put Job to the test, first by touching only his outer life. In one day, Job lost all his thousands of livestock and servants to both human and divine disaster, one right after the other. Poof . . . gone. Then, horror of horrors, all ten of his children died at the same time when the house they were in collapsed in a mighty storm. At that point Job showed nothing but faith: **"Naked I came from my mother's womb, and naked I will depart. The Lord gave and the Lord has taken away; may the name of the Lord be praised"** (1:21).

Satan came back to God with another test: "Skin for skin! Sure, he still trusts you—he doesn't really feel any personal pain. But strike his flesh, and he'll curse you to your face" (see 2:4,5). Again God permitted him the right to afflict Job—this time including the man's body but sparing his life. Satan afflicted Job with agonizing sores all over his body, from the top of his head to the soles of his feet. It was all Job could do to sit miserably among the ashes of his fire and scrape his festering sores with a piece of broken pottery.

Have you sat with Job before? Your grief may look different from his, and maybe you're inclined to say, "I thought I had something to cry about. But look at him!" I wonder if that isn't the reason why God allowed Job to hurt so badly; he is every man's example of sorrow. When it comes right down to it, grief comes with every kind of loss we face. It can be the loss of our husband or wife or parent or child

When it comes right down to it, grief comes with every kind of loss we face.

or brother or sister. It can be the loss of the job we had for 30 years, the marriage we had dreamed of, the sight we once enjoyed when we looked in the mirror, our youthful athletic abilities, the dog or cat we shared a house with, our purpose in life, the affection of a friend or lover, the possessions we got attached to, the health we valued. Every blessing from God becomes a source of excruciating pain when it vanishes.

Wrestling With God

The next 35 chapters of Job's account record the inner struggles that Job felt as he tried to figure out, in a discussion with four friends, why all this was happening to him. Nothing made sense. God had all power; Job loved him and sought to serve him with all his heart. God must be unfair to let these events unfold. "If I've done wrong to God or man, I should have this coming. But that's not the case," Job said in the first 34 verses of chapter 31. **"I sign now my defense—let the Almighty answer me; let my accuser put his indictment in writing"** (31:35). In other words, "Just put me in a courtroom with my God, and I'll show him he was wrong!"

About this time, a storm came from the north and God spoke to Job out of the storm: **"Who is this that obscures my plans with words without knowledge? Brace yourself like a man; I will question you, and you shall answer me"** (38:2,3). Over the next four chapters—the longest direct discussion God from heaven had with a man on earth in the entire Bible—the Lord reminded his man Job how little he really knew about God, his power, his creation, his wisdom, and his ways. He never really answered Job's question, "Why, Lord?"

declared, "'My thoughts are not your thoughts, neither are your ways my ways,' declares the LORD. 'As the heavens are higher than the earth, so are my ways higher than your ways and my thoughts than your thoughts'" (55:8,9).

And Paul the apostle of Jesus praised God to his friends in Rome: **"Oh, the depth of the riches of the wisdom and knowledge of God! How unsearchable his judgments, and his paths beyond tracing out! 'Who has known the mind of the Lord? Or who has been his counselor?'"** (Romans 11:33,34).

Have you tried to be God's counselor? I know I have. We love to say to God, "Lord, I've got my life planned out here in a neat little box. Now all you've got to do is come down here and fit your work into my little box and everything will be just fine." But the Lord may just answer, "I've got a box of my own—and it's far better than yours." The reformer Martin Luther liked to say that ours is a "hidden God." **"Truly you are a God who has been hiding himself, the God and Savior of Israel,"** Isaiah declared (45:15). Behind a mask of events that often look contradictory and nonsensical to human eyes hide the wisdom and power of an infinite and gracious God. I may be able to offer some counsel to my fellow human beings; but when it comes to God and his wisdom for my life, I'll be far better off receiving his counsel than giving it back to him.

God knows more than we do.

God can do all things. What an awesome thought! That means that God could have prevented your loved one from dying . . . or your health from failing . . . or your job from ending . . . or your child from rebelling . . . or your depression from setting in . . . or your spouse from leaving . . . or your income from diminishing. If he permits some sorrow to flood your life, then comfort your heart with the knowledge that your Lord knows more than you do and in his knowledge he chose to use his power in a way that fits into his plan, even if it doesn't seem right to you.

It's Okay Not to Know

Job gained a huge blessing from the sorrows he endured and the answer he received from God. Job continued: **"You said, 'Listen now, and I will speak; I will question you, and you shall answer me.' My ears had heard of you but now my eyes have seen you. Therefore I despise myself and repent in dust and ashes"** (Job 42:4-6).

He had wanted to know the answer to his question, "Why, God? Why did you let me hurt so much?" as if, in knowing the answer, he would be able to make sense of his life and sorrows and find some peace. But God wanted to give him something better: a vision of God himself. "My ears had heard of you," Job said. He had heard a few things about God, passed down from his forefathers, much like we've heard a few things about Thomas Jefferson or Abraham Lincoln in an

American history class. But what an honor it would be to actually see these men face-to-face!

"But now my eyes have seen you." What an honor it was for Job to see God in action, to experience his guiding hand in his life as if one-on-one! Now he had come to understand the depth of God's perceptive involvement in the affairs of his life and to see God's deeper purpose of humbling him and calling him into a more intense relationship of trust with his Maker than ever before. Job had come to understand that his only responsibility in this earthly life was to repent of his sins and put trust and confidence in his Redeemer-God.

> **Happiness is not found in dragging God down to our level of thinking.**

I confess that I also wanted to know the *why* of our sorrows. "Why, Lord, did you let this happen? Show me that this makes sense. I tried to be a good dad to Nathan, as well as a good son of yours. It shouldn't have turned out this way. Can you somehow make it clear to my way of thinking that any good could come out of this tragedy?"

Happiness is not found in dragging God down to our own level of thinking. Instead, we find it in allowing him to draw us to a place of trust in his ways.

Think of a little baby in his mother's arms. He doesn't begin to fathom this immense, lovely creature who is holding him. She is 12 or 15 times his size, her brain weighs more than his leg, and she has a lifetime of 25 or 30 years of experience she brings to her mothering. You know where he finds his happiness and security? Not in understanding her unfathomable ways but in her familiar smell, in the reassuring voice he has been listening to during the nine months of his formation, in the warmth of her flesh next to his, and the cuddling of her arms. He just wants to be close to her, and then he can stop crying.

God compares you to being like a little child. That's not an insult but a comforting encouragement in your life of faith. The psalmist said, **"My heart is not proud, Lord, my eyes are not haughty; I do not concern myself with great matters or things too wonderful for me. But I have calmed and quieted myself, I am like a weaned child with its mother; like a weaned child I am content"** (Psalm 131:1,2).

You don't need to be in charge; you don't have to be in the know. It's okay not to see the whole picture or be in charge of the events of your life. It's enough that you can smell the smell of God, hear his reassuring voice, feel the warmth of his love in his Son, Jesus. I take great comfort in knowing that my Father in heaven knows exactly the pain I'm feeling. He knows what it's like to lose his own Son—not to some adolescent misjudgment but to an intentional act of sacrifice for the sake of a planet full of sinners. That immense love frees us up to simply cuddle close to him in his words of promise: **"Be still, and know that I am God"** (Psalm 46:10).

———

We love the mountaintops; and by God's grace, we will continue to climb many of them in our lives in this world, despite the sorrows we have had to undergo. But God may wisely determine that we need the blessing of a valley so that his kind of lasting fruit may grow and thrive. When he chooses to lead you into that valley, go there with the assurance of God's Lamb, who said, **"Even though I walk through the darkest valley, I will fear no evil, for you are with me; your rod and your staff, they comfort me"** (Psalm 23:4).

Grief Changes Me
for the Better

Years ago I attended the funeral of a teenager whose life was ended tragically. I recall speaking to the boy's parents, both of whom were reeling from their loss. The boy's mother made this statement: "I will never be the same." She was right, of course. We are shaped and changed by the events of our lives like wood on a lathe is shaped and formed by the sharp tools that touch its surface as it spins; they affect the ways we think and act, and because of the grief she had just begun to experience, she would be a different person. How could she be the same?

I don't know if she was thinking at the time that being different might actually be a good thing. I suspect not. In my own grief, it was difficult to imagine that the horrors I was experiencing in the days and weeks and months following Nathan's death could actually result in personal blessings

In God's hands, grief can change us.

for me, Connie, and my family. All I knew is that it felt like a piece of my heart had been torn out.

Now, after some time, I believe that in God's hands grief can change us, and does change us—for the better. That's another blessing that he's brought out of my own pain. Let me share with you the kinds of good things I see God working in me through my loss. I pray it will encourage you as you suffer griefs of your own.

About Change

Before we consider those changes, let me make a couple observations about change.

God is in the business of changing people. In other words, change is a good thing. The chief word in the Bible describing the way humans react positively to God's unfailing love is the word *change*. (It's actually the word *repent*. In Hebrew it carries the picture of turning around from the way we are heading and walking back to God. In Greek it means a change of mind in the way we are looking at God and treating him. Both require that things can't stay the same once we've seen God's love for sinners in action.)

Nobody likes change. Change is uncomfortable, often painful. But we all believe that change is good, don't we? Think of a little newly delivered baby brought back from the hospital. She weighs 7 pounds and is 20 inches long—perfect for her age. Her parents absolutely adore her and accept those measurements as being just right for her. But if two months later she's still 7 pounds and 20 inches long, both they and the doctor start getting concerned. Why is she still the same size? What's wrong? Shouldn't she be changing, growing? So, too, life is a series of changes—physical, emotional, and spiritual. Only when we get to heaven will we be so perfected that we won't need constant developing and changing.

Another observation: Grief doesn't necessarily change someone for the better. You may know of someone who, in his or her sorrow, has become sullen, morose, or withdrawn from the world; who has become bitter and angry; who hates God; or who resents people instead of loving them. We'd agree that those changes are bad. Grief is like a hot sun hitting a field of corn. The same sun that causes some stalks to grow and thrive and produce ears of sweet corn can make other stalks dry and withered; it all depends on the root system of the corn. The man or woman whose personal root system is reaching down into the life-giving message of the gospel of peace, where the Holy Spirit is working to refresh and awaken faith, will find that grief can stimulate greater depths of trust and understanding. Grief need not destroy you, and in Christ, it won't.

Grief need not destroy you, and in Christ, it won't.

Building Faith

Here's the first change I've seen as I stare in the mirror of my sorrows: Grief makes me rely on God even more.

Like many Christians, I've always felt like I had a pretty strong faith. I prayed. I trusted God entirely to forgive my sins. I found delight in worshiping him. I could honestly say that I enjoyed serving him. I talked about him with my wife and children and neighbors. If someone had asked me, "Rate your faith in God on a scale of one to ten," I suppose I would have put it pretty high—at least a seven or eight.

Then my grief hit me like a semitruck on a freeway.

In the most intense sorrow of my life, I was forced to ask—I mean really, *really* ask—do I trust God, or don't I? Is he just the subject of well-formulated creeds that I have put to heart, or is he the one who **"has done everything well"** (Mark 7:37), who **"neither slumbers nor sleeps"** (Psalm 121:4), who **"is my rock and my salvation"** (Psalm 62:2)?

The examples we see in Scripture show us pointedly that God uses hard times—call them crises—to nudge his children to deeper levels of trust in him. Think of Jonah, the reluctant missionary, who, while running away from God, was thrown overboard into the Mediterranean Sea during a storm. As he sank down into the depths and felt seaweed wrapping itself around his head, he turned to the only One who could help him. He reflected (from inside a big fish—quite a place to consider one's faith): **"In my distress I called to the LORD, and he answered me"** (Jonah 2:2). Isn't that something? It's not "in my comfort" or "in my security" or "in my blessings" that he called to the Lord, his Savior-God of free and faithful

God uses hard times to nudge his children to deeper levels of trust in him.

love, though he no doubt had plenty of them in his life too. We typically don't grow in faith when life is humming along smoothly. The bumps in the road reveal the creaks and groans of the car's manufacture and call for the repairs that ultimately make the car better, stronger, more reliable.

Another example is found in the words of the prophet Zechariah. God says of his wandering people, **"I will refine them like silver and test them like gold. They will call on my name and I will answer them; I will say, 'They are my people,' and they will say, 'The Lord is our God'"** (13:9).

Maybe you've been to a silver mine like I have. It's a bit of a shock the first time to see that silver doesn't come out of the ground looking nice and shiny. In fact, it looks a whole lot like ugly dirt and stone, only slightly lighter colored. It needs a huge amount of refining to make the silver into the stuff that bracelets and earrings are made of. That refining isn't done by taking a gentle cloth and rubbing it over the surface of the ore. Instead the ore must be violently crushed and recrushed, then burned and reburned in thousands of degrees of heat until the impurities are removed and all that remains is the lovely silver.

Peter said much the same thing to his generation. Writing about the persecutions and sorrows his readers were facing, he said, **"These** (grief in all kinds of trials) **have come so that the proven genuineness of your faith—of greater worth than gold, which perishes even though** refined by fire—may result in praise, glory and honor when Jesus Christ is revealed" (1 Peter 1:7).

Zechariah and Peter remind us that building faith is a lot like ore refining. At first it's full of impurities and actually looks a lot like the world around it. But run it through the ore crusher of sorrows and the fires of affliction and then watch it become shiny and bright. Listen as it learns to say with ever greater confidence, "The Lord is my God." I can trust him, especially when I hurt, to bless me and make my faith better, stronger, more unwavering. It's the best kind of gift God can give to people who are saved by grace, through faith.

I can trust him, especially when I hurt, to bless me.

Teaching Compassion

A second change God works through sorrows takes the form of the way we view and treat others.

I have a confession to make here. I'm not the most compassionate or empathetic person in the world. I have a way of being able to segment out scenes of suffering and sorrow in others and say to myself, "That's not my issue." Using a biblical analogy, it's frighteningly possible for me to be the priest or the Levite who passed on the other side of the road by the man who was attacked by robbers, left bleeding and dying. I don't like that inhuman side of me.

I believe that through my own grief God

24

has been making me more compassionate and sympathetic toward others in their sorrows. Has that happened to you too?

St. Paul said, **"Praise be to the God and Father of our Lord Jesus Christ, the Father of compassion and the God of all comfort, who comforts us in all our troubles, so that we can comfort those in any trouble with the comfort we ourselves have received from God"** (2 Corinthians 1:3,4).

Do you get that? The comfort God gives us in the midst of our troubles has the special purpose of equipping us to comfort others who are going through similar troubles. The woman who has felt the agony of a miscarriage may be the best one to comfort another woman who has lost her unborn child. The divorcé can offer God's strength most powerfully to another on the brink of losing his or her marriage dreams.

A woman once reflected that when someone told her, "I'm depressed," she used to say, "Oh, I'm sorry to hear that." That is, until she went through a long period of deep, dark depression herself—the kind where you wake up crying, cry all day, and go to bed with tears. Now when someone says, "I'm depressed," she says, "Oh no, I'm so, so sorry. Can we talk?"

After my son died, we received a letter from someone several states away whose son had likewise taken his own life a year before. She wrote, "You have joined an elite club that you did not want to join, but we understand your pain and want you to know that, with God's help, you will heal and you will smile again." It was comforting to hear this from someone who had been there before us.

Now it's our turn. We are wondering whether the Lord will use us, as he sees us through this grief, to offer special support to other parents who have lost children by suicide, maybe by starting a support group. Our hearts bleed for others whose lives have been touched by such pain. It could be that our son's death has served to awaken those emotional nerve endings that will put me in closer touch with the pain and sorrow so many others have endured, with the final purpose of being a greater servant to my sorrowing brothers and sisters out there. Thanks, Lord, for making me more human, more willing to mourn with those who mourn.

Sadness Can Be Good

Ever since the Declaration of Independence was penned, we Americans have been keenly aware of those inalienable rights of life, liberty, and the pursuit of happiness. As a culture, we have often pursued happiness with a passion. In fact, we think there's something wrong if we don't have happiness in our lives.

This may sound kind of crazy, but have you ever considered that having sadness in your life might be a *good* thing? I believe our sorrows have a way of reminding us of this. It's a change in thinking that the Lord has led me to appreciate during our time of tears. Here's the change:

Grief keeps me from the foolishness of seeking happiness.

Solomon, the wise king of Israel, reflected on the lessons the Lord had taught him during his many years on earth. As an old man, he made this statement about sorrow versus happiness: **"It is better to go to a house of mourning than to go to a house of feasting, for death is the destiny of everyone; the living should take this to heart. Frustration is better than laughter, because a sad face is good for the heart. The heart of the wise is in the house of mourning, but the heart of fools is in the house of pleasure"** (Ecclesiastes 7:2-4).

"A sad face is good for the heart"? Solomon, surely this is a mistake; you meant a *happy* face is good for the heart, right? That's my knee-jerk reaction to his words. But he made no mistake. Years of watching humans convinced him that the world is full of fools looking for some kind of happiness "under the sun" (that is, without a God— and heaven-focused view of things). They are running to bars and night clubs and comedy channels trying to

The only happiness that will last is the one whose roots and author are in heaven.

find more reasons to laugh. And they miss the big points God is teaching them: 1) That this world has been infected with sin and death; 2) That this world cannot be a place of lasting happiness, ever since the curse pronounced on man's sin in Genesis chapter three; 3) That the only happiness that will last is the one whose roots and author are in heaven.

This world, meanwhile, is mainly a place of sorrow; the psalmist famously called it a "vale of tears" (Psalm 84:6—the NIV translation uses the Hebrew word *Baca*, literally meaning "weeping"). That doesn't mean we can't or won't enjoy some happiness here. But we have a clear understanding that sorrow is a part of our lives in a sinful world. And God can use this sorrow to bless our faith. Hymn writer Paul Gerhardt penned the truth when he wrote this:

God gives me my days of gladness,
And I will trust him still when he sends me sadness.
God is good; his love attends me
Day by day, come what may, guides me and defends me.

Going to the hospital room of someone who has suffered a serious accident or visiting someone who now is in a hospice, ravaged by cancer, or spending time in a funeral home with the family of someone whose loved one has left this "valley of Baca" or enduring the terrific, dark sorrow that you personally may be undergoing because you have lost someone or something precious to you . . . these are good and important for us as children of God and citizens of this temporary, worldly kingdom. Solomon was right; wisdom resides in the house of mourning. If the Lord permits you to dwell in that house for a time, you will not be the same. You will be wiser, better, and more understanding about the things that don't matter here and things that do matter eternally. Do not turn away from the periods the Lord asks you to spend in such a house.

Much Is Right

Enduring the pain of grief can seem to be entirely purposeless. Days turn into weeks and into months of gray days, muted music, and blank stares. Nothing seems to matter much anymore. Occasionally, the sorrow lets up, but more often it seems to oppress and overwhelm the spirit like the waves and breakers that crash against the shore. Tears and sobbing ensue.

Then a beam of sunshine breaks through the clouds, and it strikes me how much is actually going *right*. My wife, who weeps at my side, still loves and supports me. I have three beautiful children who are still with me, giving me much joy. My church stands by my side and encourages me. I have a comfortable house to live in, food to eat, and a dependable car to drive, evidence of the Lord's faithful care. Best of all, the Lord has given me his gospel of peace, which assures me that, for Christ's sake, my sins are gone. Gone! Washed away in the blood of the Lamb of God, who takes away the sins of the world. Because of that, the Lord of heaven and earth is on my side, promising that he is actively working together all things for the sake of me, his dear child. There is nothing to separate me from his love, not even Nathan's seemingly senseless death.

Maybe that's why this simple Bible refrain is so powerful: **"Give thanks to the Lord, for he is good. His love endures forever"** (Psalm 136:1).

God is the good one. His steadfast love keeps flowing down, even in the darkest moments of our personal losses and despair. A stone in the shoe of a hiker may cause overwhelming pain, but it doesn't cancel out the beauty that surrounds him; nor should he let it. Can we let the terrible loss we feel cancel out the thousands of glorious blessings that God showers down from heaven every moment of this life we've learned to call "a time of grace"? God forbid.

———

"I will never be the same," says the grief-stricken mother. I agree. I can never be the same either, but maybe that's not a bad thing. The God we worship is so amazingly gracious, so fantastically powerful, that he can bring good out of evil and change us in ways that will bless us. That's one of his great blessings that comes out of grief. Lord, please change me—for the better.

I Can Live Without Anything, Except Jesus

Years ago, Dr. Elisabeth Kübler-Ross published a book that became widely known in the study of human grief called *On Death & Dying*. In it she identified five different "stages" of grief that seem to be common to humankind whenever anyone suffers a severe emotional loss. They don't necessarily happen in this order, but they do tend to happen. They include:

- **Denial** (This isn't *happening* to me!)
- **Anger** (Why is this happening to *me*?)
- **Bargaining** (I promise I'll be a better person *if* . . .)
- **Depression** (I don't *care* anymore.)
- **Acceptance** (*I'm ready* for whatever comes.)

Why do so many seem to go through these stages or aspects of grieving? There is a tangible sense that we have lost something that's terribly important to us and we desperately want it back. We can't imagine going on through life without the person or the mode of living that we had become used to. If someone had told my wife and me before it happened that we would lose a child, we would have recoiled from the thought. "No! Impossible! Can't happen to us!" we would have said. But it did.

I used to be so amazed when I'd talk to older folks in nursing homes and learned all the terrible griefs they had had to suffer during their lives—

children who died in war, spouses who left them, sicknesses they endured, poverty they overcame— and yet it seemed they could talk so matter-of-factly about it! What was wrong with these people? Why didn't they break down and weep? Did they have hearts of stone?

Or is it just that they had learned the lesson that I'd like to share with you next: I can live without anything, except Jesus?

Grieving With Hope

There's no biblical reason to insist you have to be a Christian to go through the various stages of grieving and even get to that last one, acceptance, successfully. But we Christians have a special resource at our disposal and a special reason for getting there more quickly. We know our Lord and Savior. We've heard his promises, and he has given us hope that the rest of the world cannot understand or even dream of. That's what St. Paul was saying when he urged his friends in Thessalonica, **"Brothers and sisters, we do not want you to be uninformed about those who sleep in death, so that you do not grieve like the rest of mankind, who have no hope. For we believe that Jesus died and rose again"** (1 Thessalonians 4:13,14).

Grieve, Friend, by all means grieve. Don't cover up what's happening inside you with a mask of pretense. Allow yourself the right to work through the pain and sorrow that is such a real part of facing your loss. But when you do so in Christ, realize that you face your sorrow with something that much of the world doesn't enjoy. You've got **_You've got Jesus._** Jesus, with his death and resurrection, his power and love. You've got hope.

Much I Can Live Without

We live in a beautiful material world. God created it! He surrounds us with good things he uses to feed us, cloth us, shelter us, and please us in hundreds of ways. That includes people blessings too—our family members, friends, neighbors, men and women we work with. They all are woven together into a lovely tapestry of our lives that shapes us and defines us.

But sometimes that tapestry starts to take over our lives, and we begin to treat the gifts with which God surrounds us with the same honor and desire we ought to be giving God. That gets us into trouble. It's like the story of an African tribe that had learned to capture a certain monkey by its own greed. The hunters found a hollow log and carved a hole in it just big enough for a monkey to stick its hand into it. Then they put some seeds into the hollow log that would tempt the monkey. The animal saw the seeds and stuck its hand into the hole, grabbing the seeds. But the fist the monkey was making made it impossible for the monkey to get its hand out of the hole. And the monkey was so foolish that it refused to let go of the seeds even when the hunters came along and grabbed it.

People make a deadly fist too. They grab on to the money, the possessions, the people whom the Lord puts into their lives as if they were God himself. They commit idolatry without even realizing it. It traps them and ultimately will destroy them.

Grief has a way of helping us loosen our grip on the things that consume us.

I think of a woman I once counseled who was full of anxiety to the point that she could hardly even sleep at night. She had lost her father in the past year—the man whom she had adored and from whom she had sought much direction, advice, and comfort in her adult life. Now that he was gone, she felt lost and alone, even though she was happily married. When I suggested to her that the kind of trust she had been placing in her father was the same kind of trust God asks us to put in him, she was stunned. She realized she had been treating her father as if he were God. Now her "god" was gone, and she was traumatized. Only by repenting of her overreliance on her father and putting her faith in the God who said, "Never will I leave you; never will I forsake you" could she begin to sleep in peace again.

It was her grief that finally helped her let go of

a person who, for all the blessing he had brought to her life, was not God.

There's a reason why our Savior and Lord warned each of us, **"Anyone who loves their father or mother more than me is not worthy of me; anyone who loves their son or daughter more than me is not worthy of me. Whoever does not take up their cross and follow me is not worthy of me. Whoever finds their life will lose it, and whoever loses their life for my sake will find it"** (Matthew 10:37-39).

Nathan's death brought Connie and me face-to-face with this issue. Could it be that I loved the presence of my son in my life even more than I loved my God, who shared him with me for 16 years? Could it be that I'm inclined to "find" my life in my role as a father or husband or pastor or friend more than I find it in the security of being a child of God and a willing servant of the King? Am I willing to lose the things that tend to give me a false sense of security—my "life"—if the Lord who is my life determines that his will is to permit me to lose one or more of them?

Can I ask you a personal question: What is the one thing you believe deep down you could not survive without? Is it your spouse . . . your parent . . . your child . . . your health . . . your wealth . . . your looks . . . someone's love . . . a close friendship . . . your dreams . . . your retirement? Let me give you encouragement. If the Lord takes something away from you, he will give you the grace to open up your fist and let go. Through your loss, he may bless you with a wonderful awareness that you can live without anyone or anything except your Savior Jesus.

One Thing Is Needed

That leads us to an important point that Jesus made when he was with his dear friends Mary and her sister, Martha. Remember how Martha was in the kitchen, busily preparing a meal for Jesus and his friends, while Mary sat in the living room listening to Jesus teaching her? Martha became frustrated. **"Lord, don't you care that my sister has left me to do the work by myself? Tell her to help me,"** she scolded. Jesus answered, **"Martha, Martha, . . . you are worried and upset about many things, but few things are needed—or indeed only one. Mary has chosen what is better, and it will not be taken from her"** (Luke 10:40-42).

"Only one thing is needed," Jesus said to his good friend, who for a moment had taken her eyes off the thing in life that really mattered. Only one—not three, not even two. To have Jesus is to have everything you need for body and life. Do you believe that?

For a while the God-fearing worship leader of Israel didn't. His name was Asaph. He looked about at the world around him and began to notice that, compared to the godless people around him, he seemed to be on the short end. They were healthy and strong. They had money and fun. They prospered. People looked up to them and came to them for advice and wisdom. But what did he have? Seemingly nothing of value. He suffered a grief of his own—the kind of grief that comes when you get to the point of a so-called midlife crisis, wondering if your life really counts for much. Many of your dreams are unfulfilled, and it looks like you're on the down slope instead of moving ahead.

Asaph admitted that during this time of loss and grief, it changed his heart for the worse: **"When my heart was grieved and my spirit embittered, I was senseless and ignorant; I was a brute beast before you"** he said (Psalm 73:21,22). He had become like a material-centered animal, completely forgetting the grace and mercy of his God. Grief can do that to you; all you feel is loss; all you feel is sorrow. The object of your affection is gone.

But God revealed a great insight to him in his grief: **"Yet I am always with [God]; you hold me by my right hand. You guide me with your counsel, and afterward you will take me into glory. Whom have I in heaven but you? And earth has nothing I desire besides you. My flesh and my heart may fail, but God is the strength of my heart and my portion forever"** (Psalm 73:23-26).

Asaph was reminded that the one thing that mattered most would never be taken from him. His Lord and Savior was by his side, for ever and ever. Like a father taking his little child by the hand, God took Asaph by his hand and would not let go—ever. In this life, that same God would give him dependable guidance and advice through his Word, leading him every step of the way. When his days on earth were completed, his loving God would take him out of this world to his glorious home in heaven. How rich was his inheritance as the son of the King!

No wonder Asaph could say, "Earth has nothing I desire besides you." Flesh, world, heart may fail. Happiness may dissolve into tears and sorrow. Dear friends and loved ones may depart, but God will never fail. All the magnificence, attractiveness, comfort, and security God built into this world of ours ultimately has no grip on the heart of God's child who finds his real desire "beyond the sun" in the realms of heaven.

There is nothing we need more desperately than his love, his gospel of peace.

Jesus is *everything*! He left his heavenly Father's home to join us in our weary journey on earth. He came, the bringer of a new and lasting kingdom of grace and hope. He took our place as the provider of perfect righteousness through a faultless performance of God's holy will. He bore our guilt and sorrows with perfect innocence, carrying them on his holy shoulders to the cross of Calvary. On the third day after his death, he did the impossible and defeated death and the grave with a head-on, face-to-face confrontation and came out the victor, championing resurrection for the entire planet and pronouncing all people not guilty in the sight of God Almighty. There is no issue on earth more central than this one. There is nothing we need more desperately than his love, his gospel of peace.

I'm sure you've seen the bumper sticker that reads: "Know Jesus, know peace; no Jesus, no peace." It's a pointed reminder that Jesus was right: Only one thing is needed, and that's Jesus himself. To know him in a relationship of trust is to know lasting peace—with God, with our own hearts, with the circumstances of life that surround us. Without him, nothing you have, even the most precious of earthly gifts, makes any difference at all.

———

So go ahead, world and Satan. Take away the most precious gifts I have in this life. I may get sad or afraid; I may weep for a while in my loss. But you've really taken nothing from me. I've learned that I can live without anyone or anything, except Jesus. He will never leave me, ever. **"God is the strength of my heart, and my portion forever"** (Psalm 73:26).

Heaven Looks Better Than Ever

When was the last time you seriously thought about heaven? I mean, seriously—when you crave it, like you would crave the most precious things in your life, when you fantasize what it might be like, when you can't take your mind off it because it has become almost an obsession? If you're like most people, I bet it wasn't recently. There's too much going on. You've got ball games to go to, bills to pay, people to visit, résumés to write, trips to plan, meals to shop for, sick children to tend, books to read. You've got life to live!

It's not surprising that we tend to spend more time and thought energy on the here and now; even that is a blessing from God, having a busy, productive life. But while a busy life can be satisfying in its own way, it's got at least one downside: We tend to take our eyes off the biggest issue of all. What happens when it's all over?

The Lord has been teaching me something as I grieve that's precious. That maybe I've allowed my life to get a little too busy. That maybe it's time to sit back and ponder a bit about what really counts. Grief has a way of doing that—of making me think about where it all ends up for us Christians—in heaven.

I can think of a reason why grieving does this to a person. Grief is a persistent little man wearing a black top hat and a rumpled jacket. You wake up in the morning, and he's sitting on your sofa. You go to the office, and he rides next to you in your car. You travel but find that he likes traveling with you. You get home after a hard day, only to find that he's still sitting on your sofa. The next day is exactly like the last. You can't escape him. Some days he's quieter, smaller, less obtrusive than others, but make no mistake: he's always there. No matter how enjoyable something might be to you, he has a way of diminishing the laughter. No matter how good the food is, it doesn't taste quite the way it should. No matter how treasured the company, the little man just gets in the way of what used to be a great get-together.

Grief makes you begin to ask, "Is there something better awaiting me?" Good news, Christian. There is!

In this section, I invite you to do what Paul invites us to do in Colossians 3:1: **"Set your hearts on things above, where Christ is, seated at the right hand of God."** Think about heaven. Enjoy the truth that, in your grief,

Grief makes heaven look better than ever.

the Lord is directing your heart to your ultimate destiny in Christ, your eternal home. Grief makes heaven look better than ever.

Outwardly Decaying, Inwardly Renewed

Let me turn your attention to St. Paul's words in chapter 4 of 2 Corinthians: **"Therefore . . . we do not lose heart"** (verse 16). *Therefore* is one of those "pointer" words. Paul's just gotten done making an important point. What is it? You can read it for yourself (2 Corinthians 4:13-15). He's reminded his Corinthian friends, "You've got a unique and precious faith to talk about now that you know Jesus Christ. You believe that God raised Jesus from the dead—amazing!—and that he will also raise you one day and take you to heaven forever." No wonder we don't lose heart. No matter how painful life becomes, with its sicknesses, sorrows, disappointments, and heartaches, Easter morning fills us with hope that one day the sun will shine again, the pain will be gone, and we'll be forever in bliss with our Savior. Christians are uniquely tough because of that vivid hope.

Paul goes on: **"Though outwardly we are wasting away, yet inwardly we are being renewed day by day"** (verse 16). What a contrast he draws. Outwardly, especially as we look in the mirror, we are realizing that our bodies and lives are on a crash course with the grave. It may just be that we're getting older. Our hair is thinner and grayer. Our skin is more wrinkly and thin. Our brain or knees or organs don't work the way they were designed anymore. Our muscles ache. It may be that we're facing disease and illness. Spiritually, it may be that we're carrying the regret of an earlier sin that has profoundly affected our lives. Our sorrows are steadily wearing down the optimism about life we once had. We're hearing the tick, tick, tick of the clock of our mortality. We're on the slow, steady march to the end of this life.

We don't like that march, and we may be fighting it. But no matter how hard we fight, we lose! We run to the athletic club, but it's not quite the same as we felt a few years ago. We color our hair, only to spend more money a few weeks later on the same thing. We botox our wrinkles and tuck our tummies and replace our joints and drug our imbalances, but then the next thing goes wrong. We look for happiness and find only disappointment at every turn. Moses was right when he sang in his "old man song": **"All our days pass away under your wrath; we finish our years with a moan. Our days may come to seventy years, or eighty, if our strength endures; yet the best of them are but trouble and sorrow, for they quickly pass, and we fly away"** (Psalm 90:9,10).

But . . . **"Inwardly we are being renewed day by day"** (2 Corinthians 4:16). Because of Jesus, the inside picture looks entirely different from the outside one. The inner man or woman is like a fresh little baby, smiling, pink, fat, smooth-skinned, bursting with life and hope. That person never gets old and wrinkly, because he's being renewed every day. In fact, the closer he is to the Savior and the more he is reminded of his baptism in the gospel of God's Son, the younger and fresher and more vital and knowledgeable he is as he gets older and grows up in his salvation. Joy is born, optimism is refreshed, and vision is restored. The dour march to the grave has become a race to hope and life!

Are you learning to pay less attention to what you see in your life's mirror and more attention to the inner birth that is happening within you?

Blessed, Uneven Scales

Paul paints another vivid picture for us who are caught up in our painful troubles or tearful sorrows: **"For our light and momentary troubles are achieving for us an eternal glory that far outweighs them all"** (2 Corinthians 4:17).

I'm inclined to get a bit testy with my friend Paul when I hear him say this: "Light and momentary." Paul, what do you understand of my troubles? Have you ever lost a son? You don't know the agony I've been through. Losing Nathan was like having my heart torn from my chest. How dare you make light of my grief!

And then, I must be quiet and listen. Paul is right.

Our troubles don't feel light and don't seem momentary. But Jesus knows what he's talking about when he speaks through the mouth of his apostle. The Spirit does a good job in his Word of giving us a balanced view of every heartache we endure. Psalm 30:5 says, **"For his anger lasts only a moment, but his favor lasts a lifetime; weeping may stay for the night, but rejoicing comes in the morning."**

Momentary is the right word, from God's perspective in heaven, to describe my sorrows. To me they seem unending. But my gracious Lord tells me that, compared to the joys that await me, my tears will last only for the few hours of a night. Then comes the morning, yes an eternal lifetime, of the joy of heaven.

Light is the right word too. The apostle would have us draw on the sketch pad of our minds the picture of an old-fashioned balance scale. He seems to run out of the right words in the picture; he says that the glorious joys that await us are "way, way heavier" than our present hardships. He would say that the tears we are crying, the pain we are enduring, the sorrows we are suffering add up to about 5 ounces of weight on the one side of the scale. Meanwhile, as God blesses these hardships and uses them to develop our faith and trust in him, there are 5 tons of glory and joy on the other end of the scale! Our sorrows can't be compared with our future glory; they shouldn't even be on the same scale. Paul said virtually the same thing in Romans 8:18: **"I consider that our present sufferings are not worth comparing with the glory that will be revealed in us."**

> *Compared to the joys that await me, my tears will last only for the few hours of a night.*

I wish I could always remember that, don't you? I wish I could have the childlike faith of the little girl who was taking an evening walk with her father. Wonderingly, she looked up at the stars and exclaimed, "Oh, Daddy, if the wrong side of heaven is so beautiful, what must the right side be like!"

Seeing the Unseen

Paul concludes, **"So we fix our eyes not on what is seen, but on what is unseen, since what is seen is temporary, but what is unseen is eternal"** (2 Corinthians 4:18).

This would sound crazy, even impossible, if we hadn't heard the good news of Jesus and the kingdom of grace he came to bring to the world. But thanks to Jesus' teaching and, ultimately, his work of redeeming us from our sins, we've learned to look for things that most of the world can't see. We've learned that we are able to see the unseen. We've learned to see God in the face of his one and only Son. We've learned to perceive righteousness where there was once only sin. We've learned to grasp forgiveness where before there could only be condemnation. We've learned to find comfort where others might only find sorrow.

We've learned to see heaven too with the new eyes of faith that God has given us. While others might only see the splendor of the mountains and waves, of forests and deserts, of planets and stars, our gracious Lord has opened to us the unseen splendors of our heavenly home. That view of heaven is glorious! Think, for example, of the vision St. John shared with us in the revelation he received from Jesus: **"Then I saw 'a new heaven and a new earth,' for the first heaven and the first earth had passed away, and there was no longer any sea. I saw the Holy City, the new Jerusalem, coming down out of heaven from God, prepared as a bride** beautifully dressed for her husband. And I heard a loud voice from the throne saying, 'Look! God's dwelling is now among the people, and he will dwell with them. They will be his people, and God himself will be with them and be their God. "He will wipe every tear from their eyes. There will be no more death" or mourning or crying or pain, for the old order of things has passed away'" (Revelation 21:1-4).

I can't imagine such a place on my own, especially when tears flood my eyes and sorrow overwhelms my heart. But I am glad the Lord can envision a place where I will cry no more. That's the home where I want to be. Heaven looks better than ever.

When you can see heaven by faith, it begins to change the way you live too. An anonymous writer penned a story about an American tourist's visit to the 19th-century Polish rabbi Chofetz Chaim. When he reached the famous rabbi's home, he was astonished

The Lord can envision a place where I will cry no more.

to see that it was only a simple room filled with books, plus a table and a bench.

The tourist asked, "Rabbi, where is your furniture?"

"Where is yours?" replied the rabbi.

"Mine?" asked the puzzled American. "But I'm a visitor here. I'm only passing through."

"So am I," said Chofetz Chaim.

Have you learned too that you're just a visitor

here? Are you convinced that whatever you've lost, or may lose in the future, is not really a part of the eternal treasure that the Lord has stored up for you in heaven through the gift of his Son? Can you find refuge in the knowledge that, at best, your world is just a hotel you're stopping at on the way to your real home?

Yes, by God's grace, you can!

———

The day will surely come when all grief will be but a distant memory for God's children. In the meantime, together we encourage one another with the hope given us in the arrival, the holy life, the atoning death, and the powerful resurrection of Jesus Christ, God's ultimate "I love you" to the world. I pray this book has helped you to that end.

About the Writer

Pastor Kurt Ebert has served as a pastor in Nebraska, Colorado, and Wisconsin for over 30 years. He and his wife, Connie, were blessed with four children. For the past six years, the experience with their own personal grief and God's comfort has opened doors for them to lead a monthly grief support group for others whose lives have been touched by the sorrow of suicide. It's called Wings of Hope (WingsofHopeMequon.org).

About Time of Grace

Time of Grace is for people who want more growth and less struggle in their spiritual walk. Through the timeless truth of God's Word, we connect people to God's grace so they know they are loved and forgiven and so they can start living in the freedom they've always wanted.

To discover more, please visit timeofgrace.org or call 800.661.3311.

Help share God's message of grace!

Every gift you give helps Time of Grace reach people around the world with the good news of Jesus. Your generosity and prayer support take the gospel of grace to others through our ministry outreach and help them find the restart with Jesus they need.

Give today at timeofgrace.org/give or by calling 800.661.3311.

Thank you!